Earworm

Nick Thran

NIGHTWOOD EDITIONS

Gibsons, BC • 2011

Nightwood Editions
P.O. Box 1779
Gibsons, BC VON 1VO
Canada
www.nightwoodeditions.com

Nightwood Editions acknowledges financial support from the Government of
Canada through the Canada Book Fund and the Canada Council for the Arts, and
from the Province of British Columbia through the British Columbia Arts Council
and the Book Publisher's Tax Credit.

This book has been produced on 100% post-consumer recycled, ancient-forest-free
paper, processed chlorine-free and printed with vegetable-based dyes.

TYPESETTING & COVER DESIGN: Carleton Wilson
Cover images courtesy of Wikimedia Commons & stock.xchng;
graphic elements courtesy of misprintedtype.com.

Printed and bound in Canada

LIBRARY AND ARCHIVES CANADA CATALOGUING IN PUBLICATION

Thran, Nick, 1980–
Earworm / Nick Thran.

Poems.
ISBN 978-0-88971-260-7

1. Title.

PS8639.H73E37 2011   C811'.6   C2011-900028-8

For Sue

CONTENTS

I.

II.

III.

Oh, what sound of gold going,
of gold now going to eternity;
how sad our ear, to have to hear
that gold that is going to eternity,
this silence that is going to remain
without its gold that is going to eternity!

"Sunset" by Juan Ramón Jiménez (tr. Kate Flores)

I.

HOUSE BY THE RAILROAD

Edward Hopper, 1925

"The awning looks like a piano,"
my companion said. "No, wait.
The awning looks like a rolltop desk." And so
I took up his unused instrument. Then the tracks across
the foreground began to resemble the player's bench,
and the lack of anything resembling a musician lent
an ennui to the pale blue paint
which was the same blue as the sky. Perspective
meant seeing the house from only one side of the tracks.
"I imagine myself walking toward it," I said,
"but from another painting, armed with provisions—
milk, toothpaste and the like. I'm going to live there for a time."
"I'm going there too," my companion said. "But as
the mysterious one with a dark, unspoken history.
What kind of person rents a room in a mansion that is
so close to those tracks?" I didn't answer. I was on my way upstairs
to claim the garret room with the big windows—the quietest spot
in the house, I thought; the room with the most sunlight.
At night I could hear my companion downstairs at his rolltop desk
revising documents, memoirs, notes to the people he'd left—
I couldn't say for sure. I knew so little of this man.
The train whistle would blow around 3 a.m.,
travelling a distance between two unknown points
outside of the frame. Like a hand absent-mindedly brushing keys
on the way to somewhere else, I thought. Then envy for
his rolltop desk, his second guess,
and the care he took to get it right.

TO LEAN INTO THE HANDS OF THE SECOND-PERSON PRONOUN IS ALSO A KIND OF LOVE

You have not walked the Great Wall of China,
or seen hieroglyphs on cave walls illumined

by the lamp on a hard hat; though you have moved
into purple attic rooms and painted them over.

Squirrels found their way into the walls one fall,
their scratching expanding your idea of the wall

the way Borges expands your idea of the library,
which contains the entire universe. O

wrecking ball, the eye that sees straight into
the fragile nature of these walls! You have friends

who build walls around themselves, others
who live so exposed that you fear for their safety.

A neighbour's OMs would reverberate through the walls
every night at eleven o'clock, and you felt peace

by proximity. Despite screaming through walls
and crying through walls. Despite waking in the middle

of the night to an ecstatic shriek so fierce you sprang
into action, believing someone in serious danger

on the other side of the wall. Shooting guard Ray Allen
once scored fifty-one points on a big-screen television

and you cheered till they closed the pub down
and the screen went concrete grey. Then a cigarette outside

against a wall with a man who tells you his daughter
was murdered by dealers for a debt he could not pay.

These are the walls that shelter your family.
These are the walls that shelter your hamster.

The thin bars through which you admire her
are as rigid as stanzas of Rilke's "Der Panther."

Animals enclosed in artificial space
often bunch into the corners. *The Wall*

is an album by Pink Floyd which
you're proud to be able to finally admit

is *terrible* now that you are not stoned
in your friend's basement at age fourteen

trying your best to create an aura of coolness
by agreeing with everything they say is "wicked"

until you have built a whole wall of what's "wicked"
made of things you can't remember now

or just won't bother to list, barriers to the future,
to the points up ahead you must constantly hurdle

as if motion itself keeps the hurdles unthreatening,
hurdles themselves a kind of prepubescent wall.

If you carve *carpe diem* into a park bench
someone will dig in until it reads *carp*per*diem*.

If you hang a painting someone might say
the angle looks all wrong. A firing squad

leaves trickles of blood on the bricks
just as grandmother paints a hummingbird

at the bottom of the stairs. The stony nubs
of ancient cities—Troy, for instance—

rise out of the ground, the jawbones of epochs.
They talk to us, or, rather, to the archaeologists

who translate for us, and we are seldom surprised to find
the words they say are cruel. If you take your date

by surprise outside the restaurant, press her up
against the wall and kiss her hard, it is only the prelude

to a mattress, which is a softer, more forgiving wall,
of the kind we also provide for children

or the criminally insane. *Valencia, Spain, 1933*
is a "wicked" shot by a photographer, Henri

Cartier-Bresson, of a boy with eyes rolled back
who touches his hand to a wall. You've sat many hours

wondering what he is thinking. The wall itself
worn by weather and time, the paint peeled—

so much texture it looks less
like a wall than a nameless city at night

as viewed from a boat in its harbour;
and though the fact of the wall remains

he touches that fact, a hand on your lips
that says hush. I think we are nearly there.

DAVID

Caravaggio, 1600

To begin with the tenderness given to Goliath's face
is to speak of forgetting. Forget Caravaggio's painting,
for one cannot conjure it up in the midst of some other
terror. One can break it down only after this other mist
settles. This requires your survival. This requires the soil,
which breaks down the face to a fine, particulate matter.
What of the brush strokes? What of the weeds?

Let's not speak of tenderness. Burning the midnight oil
at the office on Yonge St., we were drinking beer.
My friend had been trolling the net all night. "Oh, shit,"
he said, as if to his own lack of surprise. "Get over here.
This is the site where they stream the beheadings."

Darling	*Beech wood*
Darling	*Drunk tank*
Darling	*Rose bush*
Darling	*Bank light*
Darling	*Front lawn*
Darling	*Glass lamps*
Darling	*Bathtub*
Darling	*Car park*
Darling	*Long drive*
Darling	*Deer's eyes*
Darling	*Floorboards*
Darling	*Night sweat*
Darling	*Warm bed*
Darling	
Darling	
Darling	

THE ORIGINS OF GLOSS
THROUGH THE LOGIC OF DREAMS
DURING THE TWILIGHT OF PERIODICALS

No loop-de-looping around
    the gorgeous birds

or depositing
    radioactive waste

outside the Earth's atmosphere,
    or making faces

at enemies
    through

the little oval windows.
    No:

just gliding over a
    major city,

marvelling
    at the rooftop gardens

of the tall buildings,
    like the exotic haircuts

of runway models
    from countries you've never been to.

The public
    needs to see this,

a pigeon whispers.
    We'll capture

the star-struck look
    of koi fish ponds.

Confirm which way
    each particular piece

of patio furniture leans.
    Content-wise:

softer than eiderdown,
    while still stomping around

in those leather shoes heard
    throughout the halls

of the office towers
    that once housed
    the great magazines.

Each issue will be run through
    the engine's propellers

and hit the streets
    already partially

disposed,
    putting much of our

existing readership,
    so pressed for time,

at ease. While those
    who still enjoy piecing

the issues together
    tinselled scrap

by tinselled scrap
    can

pull them off of the railings
    or out of a

co-worker's hair,
    or contemplate them

from a safe distance—
    just an added sheen

on the already shimmering
    leaves.

EDELWEISS

Edelweiss, her favourite flower.
She was sixty-one, dead from cancer.

Edelweiss is the image on Austria's
two-cent coin. The unofficial flower

of Switzerland. Her youngest has the
tattoo done in white. Run under warm water

it catches the eye.
It's hard to see it otherwise.

1.

Insect bohemian of Aesop—
drum circles through the summer while

the ant hoards
a winter's worth of food

2.

Noisy Weeds of Middle Ground
Happy Blanks
Zealot's Fears
Agents of the Muse

3.

Such reverb
in the belly of the ark
not one creature would have kept

their sanity intact

4.

The ear on a loop
of Aerosmith albums

Just stop   I'll tell you anything
Just stop

5.

It's in high temperatures
and deep exhaustion
that its pitch is in full bloom

6.

Fresh
from the long-haired weeping willow

it lands on window screens as though designed
by government robotics labs
to flush us from our rooms

7.

It thrives on its own emptiness
It never has to choose

There were ways of avoiding the pineapple,
but they were difficult, so nobody tried.
It dominated the front page news. So insatiable

was our hunger it began showing up
on the sports page, in the obituaries, the auto pages,
when it did not play, had not died,
and had we tried to drive the pineapple
it would have spiralled into the ditch.

Could the pineapple be used as an alternate fuel source?
Was the pineapple hiding a nuclear arsenal?
It seemed so happy with the ambassador's
socialite daughter. The gossip rags were alight.
Was it strung out on pineapple? Everyone
had an opinion. These were trying times.

When it was unseasonably warm, or cold,
it was because of the pineapple. When the team
from your town beat the team from my town
in the conference finals that year
it was because of the pineapple. The fix was in.
The stock market pineappled. It all made so much sense.

There were ways of avoiding the pineapple,
but they were difficult. It ripened and festered
right there in the middle of town square,
out under the desert sun, on the basement sofa where

it had been doing nothing but sleeping,
drinking Boone's Sparkling Wine
and babbling in a feverish, untranslatable tongue.

People had knelt down and prayed to the pineapple. People
had named streets and children and universities after the pineapple.
Shall I compare thee to a summer's pineapple? Shakespeare wrote
in his most famous poem, and scholars agreed pineapple
was *the* central theme of the later, more problematic plays.

So it was somewhat unexpected when it disappeared
from our consciousness, or didn't disappear so much as shrink
before our eyes into a tangible, definable, hand-held thing,
not even shrink so much as rot, not even rot so much as ripen

into a perfection we could never attain.
The shift may have happened around the end of the war,
but there was always a war going on, and if the pineapple
had been something of a pacifist, it was also the single greatest
military power on the face of the earth. People who claimed

the pineapple was like the heart now understood
it was simply a cloud that became rain that became a river
that washed into the sea. It was simply a language.
It was food and nourishment and a pillow on which
to rest your weary head. Pineapple served
at your uncle's funeral. Pineapple whispered in a lover's ear.
You could clear out your drawers, kick in the monitor
of the company laptop, leave a pineapple hanging from the light fixture
and run out the door. Nothing more would have to be said.

Removed from a snowbank the previous winter
like a tropical fish from under the ice.
Central by virtue of what the room lacked,
embers, the last licks of whatever had cleared
the rest of her things away. Brush fires
flared up throughout the Interior again that summer,
whole neighbourhoods were set ablaze.
Families lit candles for soldiers patrolling
a faraway desert. The monarch butterfly returned
in abundance, wings smearing windshields
along the country's major arteries. A friend called:
"It's a big world, Doug. Let's get you out of the house,
what do you say?" But the chair was where he chose
to sit. With no foreseeable end to our need
to control the elements, here was a fire contained.

POWER

The wind turbine's tired arms
sway at its sides. It looms over
the expressway. Over the little mouths
of the cars on the expressway.

The turbine is not your real dad.

Your real father is orbiting the earth.
Your biological father has smaller arms.
Your Father in heaven wears fabulous cuffs.

He floats on the air.
He throws cash in the air.

He waves his small arms
and he gathers it up.

II.

IN THE VICTORIAN SUBLETS OF FAILED ACTORS

The window's dark scars covered up
with pages torn from back issues
of *Empire Magazine*.

Stars of the silver screen
screen
out the elements,
the elements
work through the gloss,

yield a more acute
projection of desire:

pigeons, parked cars, telephone wires—

a twenty-four-hour feature/
collage-cum-ghost story:

this is how Glamour returns to the street.

...The time is right, in you, for some
Bold move. Now let your mother go. Now, let me come.
Horace, Bk I. 23
tr. Heather McHugh

CHLOË:

After a shift at the pub I'd take the long route back
through woods where the paths stayed damp
in the dry heat, soft soil on the slipper-thin
soles of my Chucks, the oversized headphones—

my skull slugging music from two large cups
(Black Flag, punk rock, 80 proof stuff). Away
from my mother's doting, the barflies' snickers;
where a toad is a toad is a toad is a toad. You

weren't one of those slimeballs openly eyeing
my appurtenances. *No predatory cur*, I know.
I still read through your scribbled notes.
For two thousand years the same light wind

stirs round the leaves; I've watched your "fawns" slip
their hooves through those perfectly paced little Os.

"Ocean Mist." This soap does smell like ocean mist.

So much for my threadbare shirt with its tears in the collar, its missing button, its just now barely blue.

The festival of ants is in full swing under the dome of the ant trap.

Clack of the heater.

The theme music from *Law & Order*.

When the sun angles in through the bedroom window, everything shines like a souvenir.

BELATED THANK YOU NOTE FOR THE FIBRE OPTIC
CHRISTMAS TREE YOU GAVE ME IN NINETEEN I FORGET

Light forked like water at an estuary.
Glowed like a bouquet of E.T.'s

fingertips. My roommates and I
used to sit in the dark with the thing

plugged in, map paths
through the fibreglass threads,

    and throw cans at whomever

would enter the room, flip on the
main light switch, heap so much

seeing on us at once we had to pause
and gather our bearings,

    take long, deep breaths.

Better, perhaps, in these small, measured doses.
To sidestep the watchwords that blind us:

Radiation, for instance.
Diagnosis. Wish.

The waitress is tired, but she still smiles as she pours
your coffee, so let's not send her to work
as some sort of symbol in this. Once, at a retreat
high in the mountains, forty harpists lined up together
for omelettes in the cafeteria—nubile, in long flowing dresses.
It was cinematic, like rain after a lover's quarrel, after a door
slams shut for the last time. This season my friend
has taken to calling his exes. *Just to see what they're up to,*
he says. Doesn't he already know? It's been raining for days.
The city is swarming with couples; they huddle
happily under the blooms of multicoloured umbrellas
on every single street. When the waitress swears
that she's met me before, I don't protest. Let's say
it was Norway, a year abroad. I was studying for his forensic
science exam when her breath on the back of my neck
broke through a fog, through theories and diagrams.
My name is Amanda, she said, *and I already know who you are.*

The personalities of the dwarfs
were still "open to change"
throughout the rewrites. Dopey himself
was introduced late. Why not add a Latinate
"a" to the end of his name

as Adriana Caselotti sings the Sinemet out
from the front of her cerebral cortex?

The voice of Snow White would marry a doctor
in the same year her previous husband,
the actor Norval Mitchell, died.

Pure joy will transmit as the dwarfs
remove small, bloodless jewels—

"Heigh-Ho" in the mineshaft.
Emphasis *mine*.

I have a computer. My computer hurts my eyes.
I have a fan. When I turn on my fan there is wind.
I have a painting by my sister of the human heart. My sister
works two jobs because her landlord doesn't charge
the same rent anymore.
I have a poem by Mark Strand. "Black Sea" is a wonderful poem.
I have a telephone. The captain has called me to say that I've
 won a free cruise.
I have a cup of coffee. My coffee is always finished too soon.
I have an orange chair. My orange chair is covered with clothes.
I have a dictionary. I look up the word *pusillanimous*.
I have a radio. My radio does not dream.
I have a letter from Darren. It's nice to get letters from Darren!
I have a book by Philip Gourevitch.
If I take it with me to read in bed then I will not fall asleep.

after Tomaž Šalamun

It got to be that a beaded curtain replaced each door in the dormitory. It was like moving in slow motion through the hair of a man or a woman—each room an outpost in the wilderness, a place to relax upon beanbag chairs and listen to Janis. And we desired more than the tenured nudity of the student body. Some of us kept small animals. They were like family to us. Their beady eyes jewelled the enduring smoke. And our hope was enduring, at least for those few early years. Long Gone was the name of the student president. Long Gone was the name of our humanities professor. Long Gone was the name of the janitor. He doubled as a cab driver. Had a personalized plate: GHAZAL. Left his country because his parents and siblings were murdered. Long gone, we didn't mind that the meter was going up in spectacular increments. It reminded us of the eyes of the dealer's ferret. The guy with the blue pills—wasn't Long Gone his name? Our whole outlook was going to change.

Ninja Turtles were assassins who still had the option
of cowering inside their shells.
ThunderCats told the story of a feline-blooded young swordsman
who learned to control his unwieldy phallus. I ask

what star-eyed little pecker could ever
un-fuddle the hullabaloo stirred up
by the plum-tree-in-silk figure cut
by Jessica Rabbit? Roger's tongue is still unfurling down

an endless flight of stairs. *Hello my baby! Hello my honey!*
Michigan J. Frog sang for no particular reason—no reason
a mustachioed man with an order of business
was ever going to see. If Slowpoke Rodriguez sang like that

we'd never have noticed, too busy trying to keep pace
with–*Andelé!*—Speedy Gonzalez. I still worry

for that mouse. Foghorn Leghorn breathed his dust.
And Sebastian proposed staying under the sea.

When color signifies anything, it always signifies,
as well, a respite from language and history.

As a postcard depicting an iceberg also signifies
ice cubes in a highball glass.

As a stay in a hospital—Bellevue, for instance—
signifies a respite from the debate on health care reform

to focus on one's physical state and the nature of time.
The building itself is a respite from body and time,

and a container for the passage of both
until it collapses. Bruce Springsteen sang

"57 channels and nothing on..." which
signified a respite from whatever shit

was on the radio during those days,
or at least that's how my father felt

driving his yellow Corvette at very high speeds
on the highway. His nickname then

was "the Animal," which signifies an excessive
wildness that is difficult for both the body

and time to sustain. "Gargamel"
would have been much worse,

signifying an evil wizard on the Smurfs
who signifies, as well, a very real threat

to our innocence. "Gargoyle"
would signify something *close* in sense and sound,

and, being an inanimate object, is much more still
than an animal would be

after drinking fourteen highballs and careening his car
through an empty basketball court

and into the side of some public housing.
I like to imagine the dumbstruck faces

of the strangers who had until then been sitting
in front of the TV, and my father's head

splayed over the steering wheel, cocked a bit to the left—
a position from which we may contemplate absence

and death in the paradise of the moment—
as we kids in Santa Monica

contemplated the death of puppies
in the embrace of cartoon rainbows.

It's spring inside the industrial dryer,
where a mess of towels bloom
as a single carnation, whose petals
will cover the water-slick bodies
of swimmers up from the pool.
It's spring over the porcelain bowl
between two people dining
at their local dive. The endless talk,
the shrimp wonton she holds aloft
while describing her childhood springs
in the Ozarks, or some lush place you imagine
Waits is reaching for in his gravel-dust bawler
You Can Never Hold Back Spring.

"You can never hold back spring,"
not the runoff, not the brand new smells
in the streetcar, which are only the old smells
of last spring returning, as real as sweat,
as the inward made public, as the squeak
of a box spring mattress upstairs where neighbours swear
at each other in the urgent, new tongue of the season:
You gorgeous cunt. You dirty little spring...

GLOWWORMS

Halfway down cables
in broad daylight,
critters not too proud
to crack their first beers
before noon.

Miss you. Love you.
Wish you were here.

Balloons. Balloons.
Balloons.

FOUND PSALM FOR ALTAMONT

From Stanley Booth's The True Adventures of the Rolling Stones

The Angel
with his hand
on Charlie's shoulder
was being asked
to step down
off the stage.

The Cop
told the Angel
to step down,

the Angel shook his head.
The Cop told him again
and pushed him. The Cop
had a cigarette in his mouth
and the Angel took it

out, just plucked it from between
the Cop's lips, causing the Cop to regard
the Angel with sorrowful countenance.

Charlie was playing soft rolls.
Keith was playing a slow blues riff.

The Cop
told the Angel
to step down.

"Let's play cool-out music,"
Keith said to Mick.

III.

ELECTRIC TIGER

I am going to make a tiger
— Jorge Luis Borges

In Tokyo, electric light's an afterthought.
And Vegas wears its glare like a second sweaty
skin. In Toronto, for three months, a traffic circle
homes a man-made tiger, commissioned

by the city. A gift to the kite-high late-night gawker;
electric relic; source of civic pride. For three months
traffic slows. The tiger lounges, lit-up, the opposite
of captive, while the municipal government broadcasts

warnings of an imminent city-wide energy
shortage. Janitors snuff out bank tower lights
so birds can fly through the dark columns without
smashing into the glass. We sleep in fits.

The work trucks rumble. Edison's ghost
in the shotgun seat. Please, don't take this back.

A beach bucket kicked over
hanging upside down
on the right sleeve like a bell

Storybook sea monsters

Giant crabs and cavernous shells

Frogs
the size of hammerhead sharks
A palm tree floating past our hull

An outstretched hand

Everything
quivering

How many days had I napped on deck
through my dogwatch? Killed an afternoon
over games of gin rummy?

Now Poseidon was dancing
We had to get down to the galley
Not even our Captain
could predict how long we'd be
in the ox-eye of the storm

Our ship might have been pollen
emitted from the lips
of an orchid

or the olive
sloshing back and forth
in a dry martini

Sweat
hung on in the air
like an amoebic cloud
toxic
as dark thought

O had we boarded a breaker
in the Arctic
something slow and deliberate
through silk-smooth
planes of ice

Now the power
had been cut

and we were feeling around
the unlit SS *Aloha*

for the shoulders
of friends

for the last of the fruit cocktail tins

for the hunting knives
hitched to our bootstraps

Enough about "the Blue Period."

Maybe the *Old Guitarist* was actually playing
for as long as he could hold his breath
under water. And those weren't the walls of the Parkview Arms
behind him, but the hull of a great ship,
one of those oil tankers that you can travel aboard
as a tourist, provided you don't mind the food
and stay out of the ship crew's way.

"Blue" is just one way of saying "submerged."

"Silence" is digging your feet into white sand,
extra ice please and a cocktail umbrella.

While they unload the oil drums,
you can while away time by just breathing.

You wouldn't believe the fresh air!

Monuments
Covered in snow
And bus stops
Covered in snow
And snow
Out the window
I'm trying
To quit smoking
I'm listening
To the headphones
There are people
In reflective neon vests
In the snow
They are carrying
Shovels I
Would pick this kind
Of day to start
A self-portrait I
Am Married
I am thirty
Remember
Having to get out
Of my own way
And thinking God
Was the space left
Then the space
Was a postcard
On a bulletin board

From a woman writing
Poems in a castle
In Scotland and she
Didn't even know me then
Then a husband
In a story by James Salter
Not even in the story
Any more
The smoke
Got into the bones
Said his widow
She was sexy
He was dead
He had my name
I love
My wife
I love the snow
It's like a crowd
Speaking overtop
Of my story
I dress
For the weather
I don't try to dig myself
Out from the snowy
Grave every morning
I say mean little things
Little burns sometimes
To my wife then

The space
I am
Thirty
Giddy
Perversely
Happy
Reflective neon
Hey

756*

for Barry Bonds

We had to fill him up with the feats of mythical giants—Zeus and Goliath,
"Hammerin' Hank" and "the Babe." We had to fill him up with the where-
were-you-whens? The fictitious baseball works by masters like Roth

or DeLillo. We had to fill up his trophy case, his endorsement deals.
Had to fill up the Jumbotron with his image, the ballpark with our bodies,
newspaper columns with box scores, OPSs and slugging percentages—

fill them with the details of his daily performance, considered by rights
to be in the public domain. Used him to fill awkward silences
over dinners with our partners' fathers, our granddads, clients—

inhuman feats to bring up while we ironed out our own human details.
We had to fill him up with fake wars, fake breasts, fake reports.
Fill him up with the false affirmation that men of a certain stature existed

well beyond the pale. We had to fill him up with our hard luck,
our nine-to-five jobs, our paltry salaries. Then we had to fill up his bank
account as we paid for the soaring prices of tickets, jerseys and hot dogs,

lining his pockets by filling the stands for each and every game. We had
to fill him up with scientific advances, bad advice, tough choices, then
fill him up again with what *we* would have done, the decisions our senses

of decency, respect for the game's history, would have compelled us
to make. When he didn't return the wild rounds of applause, we had to
fill him up with our loathing. We had to fill him up with test results

and government-sanctioned inquiries, just to be sure we were able
to set the record straight. And after we filled him up almost to bursting
we finally had to let him go, as a child, indifferent, lets go of a balloon

in a parking lot, and watches the asterisk
beside his own name floating away.

It's not easy for her on the phone to describe
the whales that breached metres from her off the shore.

I used to freak out at these pauses, just her breath on the line.
I used to need booze and loud music to sleep when she left

for the coast. Now, just steady rain over the roof. Bass notes
shake the windows sometimes when a car drives by.
A car drives by. Then a deep calm descends on the house.

COAST GUARD VESSEL,
PLEASURE BOAT.

Bear, lion and tiger make unlikely brothers.
Macy's fire smokes shoppers out.
Boy stuck with needles in month-long ritual.
Fatal collision of coast guard vessel, pleasure boat.

Macy's fire smokes shoppers out.
Prince William homeless for a night.
Fatal collision of coast guard vessel, unlikely brothers.
Karaoke assault suspects kicked out of court.

Prince William homeless for a night.
Conjoined twins celebrate third birthday apart.
Karaoke assault suspects kicked out of court.
Detective pulls gun during a snowball fight.

Conjoined twins celebrate third birthday apart.
Beluga gives birth for the second time in a week.
Detective pulls gun during a snowball fight.
Police catch infamous Christmas Tree Thief.

Beluga gives birth for the second time in a week.
Boy stuck with needles in month-long ritual.
Police catch infamous Christmas Tree Thief.
Bear, lion and tiger make pleasure boat.

We've been setting up the new bookstore alongside carpenters
and electricians. Dust. Most of the staff has gone down

with the flu. I've been reading Bolaño's *The Savage Detectives*
and Liz, you would love it: freewheeling young poets

barrelling through Mexico and Europe toward
an awareness, I think, that they'll have to make some other life.

The bookstore used to be an electronic repair outlet. Yesterday
a Hindu man walked in asking where the last owner was. I

couldn't tell him. The whole neighborhood is "in transition."
What does that mean? Hing's Antique Lights is going out

of business. Every day I walk by there's less and less glow
from the window. More and more silver hooks and black cords

hang like sad hairs from the walls. I've been talking with
the security alarm installer—my age—about hourly wages.

He makes twice as much as I do, and it's only temporary,
until he can get his foot in the door of the fire department

and start to fight some fires. Inspecting alarms
in a building the size of the convention centre can take

up to four months. Imagine, four months of tinkering
with panels and cameras to keep the night outside!

A fortress. While at the outskirts new signs
post mid-plot. Rebrand in the obstreperous breeze.

THE YEAR OF THE GUN

Behind the yellow tape,
watching the craned necks
of street lamps

smoke out the long night;
tiny embers
dotting King Street
seemingly all the way out

to the morning, or the country—
whichever came first. No way

to know,
and now this.

THOUGHT BUBBLES HOVERING OVER THE CANADIAN TAXIDERMISTS ASSOCIATION'S ANNUAL GENERAL MEETING

*

*Does the killdeer's head ache when a winter storm
lashes the side of the house?*

*

*These sandwiches are the white sails sent out by bread ovens
that have buoyed up my body since birth.*

*

My pastor, O pastor, how are we going to save this child?

*

Best is a line drive into the right field corner.

*

*Best is a slow morning between Genevieve's legs,
at her chest.*

*

The Bow Falls as still as a water glass.

*

*A cloud in the act of changing from
one likeness to the next.*

To sit the lived-in house and breathe its fragrant air
is to experience time in the garden of staying put.
Here are the bookshelves. Here is the wicker chair

which has practised fidelity through minor affairs
with visiting house guests. Yes, almost illicit
to sit the lived-in house. Breathing the musty air

among the layered notes of corkboards, the cat-hair
wig on the sofa, the computer monitor on sleep
and the well-fed bookshelves—the wicker chair

sags flush and contented. Folks in photos stare
at the sitter, a migratory species of insect.
To sit the lived-in house and breathe its distinct air

is to enliven the iris, snoop and browse, share
an intimacy with the owners who have lived so long with
the chattering bookshelves, their wicker chair,

that they break back into their lives by riding the getaway car
over the bare arms of the highway. What sweet kiss
to sit the lived-in house and breathe its fragrant air.
To pick from the bookshelves, lounge in the wicker chair.

I have bureaus set up in the cities she frequents.
Wired the chinchilla coat I gave as a gift
when she turned six hundred and five.
I get reports from my staff of her goings-on:
the wing-burst of kestrels in Prague,
the new neon signs in Milwaukee.
I have an accordion file full of the moments
the world has caught fire in her presence.
I must look like a drunken polka musician
late at night in my office. It's hard on our kids.
I've given up on overseeing the design
of my series of homes in the shapes of chandeliers
to hang under big city causeways and bridges.
I prefer using the payphone to using my cell.
A staffer says the smell of cinnamon is hovering
in the air in Dakar. A staffer says they spotted her
slow dancing with the butcher in Montreal,
the customers clapping, stomping and smiling.
She comes home twice a year. There's a marble sink
built into our foyer. I tell her how gorgeous she looks.
She lets me wash both of her hands.

So there's likely a more accurate name
for the glow of a deer's eyes in the dark.
For the hunger that drew a python in Florida
to swallow an alligator whole. For the aura,
the swell just before the gut burst.
For why you've been staying up late at night
on a search engine, looking for all of the possible
names for a lump at the back of your nostril.
For the name of that girl who sold you a pill
from the basket of her bike, and rode off while
her fairy wings flapped in the breeze. And a name
for that breeze. Repetune, ohrwurm,
the last song stuck in your head
which became something else. And for what else?
For not being able to say the one thing
that might have kept you from continually falling apart.
For discovering late. For replaying the video clip
of Joltin' Joe Carter's ninth-inning blast
in the '93 Series. For the sound when the ball
hit the bat, and everyone knew they'd won
before it left the park. And for the white noise
that isn't white noise, but a poor translation of what
the blood tries to say. And what the blood tries to say.
For the feeling of never wanting to leave the party
and then having to leave. For the ache in your legs
when you should have cabbed home, but decided to walk
and the walk was too far. But you had to keep on—
Earworm, Little One, chugging along, travelling towards a name.

"Raining in Darling" is the name of a song from Bonnie "Prince" Billy's album, *I See a Darkness*, Palace Records, 1999.

"I have a computer…" is after, more specifically, Tomaž Šalamun's poem "I Have a Horse," from *The Selected Poems of Tomaž Šalamun*, Ecco, 1988.

The italicized lines from "Trigger" are from Dave Hickey's essay "Pontormo's Rainbow," from the collection *Air Guitar: Essays on Art and Democracy*, Art Issues Press, 1997.

"Murder in Hawaiian Shirt" was written after Dennis Oppenheim's conceptual sculpture "Murder in Hawaiian Shirts."

"Coast Guard Vessel, Pleasure Boat" is comprised of lines from the Globe and Mail's *Watch Video* online component, around Christmas 2009.

"House by the Railroad" is for Joel Malament.

"David" is for Craig Battle and Chris Wilson-Smith.

"Queen Street" is for Elizabeth Bachinsky.

ACKNOWLEDGEMENTS

My thanks to the editors of the following publications where these poems first appeared, sometimes in earlier versions and under different titles:

Arc, The Best Canadian Poetry in English 2010, Canadian Notes and Queries, Desk Space (online), *Epiphany* (USA), *Event, The Fiddlehead, Forget* (online), *Grain, Maisonneuve, Matrix, The National Post, PRISM International, The Same* (USA), *Storyscape* (USA), *The Trinity University Review, Twaddle* and *The Walrus.*

I gratefully acknowledge the financial support of the Ontario Arts Council, the Canada Council for the Arts, New York University and the Banff Centre for the Arts.

This book has benefited enormously from the eyes and ears of some extraordinary friends, poets, editors and teachers. Thank you.

To my family (including the Sinclair branch): thanks for your support, patience, kindness and love.

Nick Thran is the author of one previous collection of poetry, *Every Inadequate Name* (Insomniac, 2006). His poems have appeared in numerous publications across Canada, including *Arc*, *The Best Canadian Poetry 2010*, *Geist*, *Maisonneuve*, *Matrix*, *The National Post* and *The Walrus*. Since growing up in western Canada, southern Spain and southern California, Nick has spent the last few years living in Toronto, Ontario and Brooklyn, New York.